the boundless bloom

the boundless bloom

vincetta

also by vincetta

metamorphosis

dedication

to all the women who have existed before
me, fully and boldly, whose frequency of
freedom reverberates through all space, time,
and dimension. whose paradigm-shifting lives
have left portals for us to leap through.

table of contents

chapter one

bone and blood

ego death for breakfast
as I feel the peak
of another psychological
purification

as I collapse
        into and
        out of
        myself
and then
        back to
myself
just in time for lunch

where moments
are spent
grounding
back into the body
back onto the Earth

just another day
of Saturn returning
me again
and again
        to and through
        myself
        until I am not
        myself
yet I am

I am
I am
I am

        —Saturn keeps returning

I find myself
 here
  yet again
praying
and hoping

to the Holy Father
to the Sacred Mother
to the one Great Spirit
that this
is the last time

feeling hopeless
and exhausted
at odds
with my sense
of power

my will
at a reckoning
with my inability
to release
control

to be here
without
the need
to wish for
something
different

to be with
my desires
without
the need
to resist
my reality

I find myself
here
yet again
struggling to
surrender

I want to fly
but I keep clipping
my wings

suspended in
space and time
neither   here
        nor there
a liminal space
between destruction
and rebirth
there is nowhere
to go
and nothing
to do
but be
and yet
my mind
is racing
fear lining
the membranes
of my brain
my muscles
weakening under
the pressure to
remain composed

—hanged (wo)man

I am
wilting
    slowly
    but surely
folding in
on myself

       —luteal

I wonder
will this ever end
these feelings
of exhaustion
        of defeat
                of feeling
utterly at the whim
of something
that seems to be
working against me
l o s t

while simultaneously
feeling renewed
        and certain
                riding the waves
of something
that seems to be
taking me exactly
where I need to be
f o u n d

I am trekking
        towards
                a new path
                a new way
two realities
being ripped
at   the   seam
my very essence
deconstructing
pieces of me
    d i s i n t e g r a t i n g
pieces of me
    coming into form

can I allow
the process

to unfold
without self
sabotaging
back to the
safeness of
the old me

thoughts
jumping sides
like ping-pong balls
rebounding against
the motherboard
of my mind
the fog of
Neptune heavy
finding stillness
to feel sane
letting the tears
clear the way
until all that
remains
is truth

—paths diverged

falling
forward
    bravely
             exposed
    uncertain
yet sure

the structures
that once
kept me warm
and safe

now a burden
bogging
me
down

I have to
let them go
the only thing
I can hold onto
is myself

deconstructing
myself
    selectively
    and intentionally
    choosing

which parts
of me can stay
    elevate and
    integrate
into a higher state

and which parts
of me must leave
    decay and
    molt
back into no-thing

the process
is somber

at times
I feel
nothing

at times
I feel
everything

at times
I feel
both
at once

what will
survive
who will
I become

I don't know
I am merely
here

slowly
spinning
through
lanes
of disdain
of pain
of old
wounds
feeling fresh
feeling new
feeling it all

memories
resurface
I plummet
submerged
back into
the past
letting it all
spill out
of me
until the well
is dry

and I am
transported
back into
the now
clear sky
open roads
something
has healed
in the
space-time
continuum

I am
crawling out
from under
the weight
of an old skin

a majority of my life
has been a resistance
a revolutionary protest
of the now

and now that the coup
has been successful
and the land of my life
is safe to occupy
I remain unsure
of what existence
is like without
the incessant fight

I have found what I
have been forging toward
but somehow feel
more lost than ever

and so I must
learn to make a
home out of peace
I must learn
to find refuge
in my body
to find safety
in my bones

and in the
way my muscles
are weighed down
to Gaia by gravity

feet touching
the sacred ground
I must learn
that there is power
in being fully

here
anchored
to the now

the body
keeps
the score
while
the mind
finds a way
to escape
the war
that rages
on inside me

I live   disconnected
    from myself
mind   and body
separate
for safety

for fear
of what I
may feel
once I make
contact
with the trauma
stored
in the memory
of my bones

knowing
one day
I must
return and
reclaim
my body
fully inhabiting
my own temple
of flesh and blood

my body
violated
more times
than I'd like to
count
my mind
pushing
running
to escape
the truth
of this
violence
afraid of
the rage
that would be
unleashed
the waves
of grief
that would
ensue
and yet
I knew
it was
the only
way through

—body reclamation

grief
found me
and became
me

every moment
my anger
was silenced
invalidated
and demonized
forced to live
as a current
under my skin

every moment
I felt fear
and swallowed
it whole
inside of
my being
buried it in
the depths
of my womb

every moment
my trust
was shattered
broken into pieces
that floated
through my vessels
longing for
wholeness

came rushing
to the doors
of my heart
awaiting to be
witnessed

calling for a
release

struggling to
find agency
in my body
when everywhere
I turn
there is an
energy of
toxic
masculinity
colonizing
patriarchy
looking to
devour
my innate
natural
feminine
power

THIS
IS
MY
BODY

I screamed
with conviction
tears filled
with the pain
of innocence lost
rolling down
my cheeks
fists pounding
into the ground
pent-up anger
reverberating into
the Earth

THIS
IS
MY
BODY

I proclaimed
through all
space
    time
and dimension
to all
past
    present
future
who have tried
to stake
their claim

THIS
IS

MY
BODY

I growled
with the fierceness
of a lioness
protecting
her cubs
as the faces
of all my
past abusers
flashed by
in the eye
of my mind

THIS
IS
MY
BODY

I declared
reassuring myself
I inhabit this body
and it is mine
not yours

THIS
IS
MY
BODY

—tantric healing

the arrogance
and ignorance
of a man
to tell me
that maybe
tantra isn't
for me

I am
the divine
feminine

I am
the mother

I am
the creatrix

I am
tantra

embodied

a rush
of emotion
commotion
explosion
volcanic
eruption

  —triggered

I have
reached the
mountain top
of a situation
that was
only a
mole hill

I have
projected
the highest
potential of
a man
onto the
limited reality
of a boy

I have
let the
limitless mosaic
of possibilities
shatter into
shards so
miniscule
that piecing
them together
is nearly impossible
nothing remains
but the rubbles
of my heart

I have
nothing left
to give but
these last
few tears
an offering
back to source

a mix of heartbreak
and gratitude
for the experience
for the loss
for the discovery
for the single
fact that
I am still here
despite
the wreckage

these last
few tears
an offering
back to
the Earth
the debris
only fertilizer
for eventual
resurrection

they used to think
Saturn was the Sun

just like
I used to think
you were the one

I wake up to a tender heart. my eyes
brimming with droplets like dew upon the
morning leaves. the moistness reminiscent of
the summer air just before the storm. my heart
aching, feeling cracked open by thunderbolts.
lightning flashes projecting visions of what my
heart yearns for across my mind's eye.

I am tired
of relationships
feeling like static
when I want them
to feel like streams

I feel a rage
I can't explain
I can't contain

my world is
collapsing
a great
black hole
has opened up
swallowed me whole
and suddenly
nothing is real
and nothing matters
because nothing
is true
but what
I feel

I become nothing
but a feeling
that encompasses
e v e r y t h i n g

I flow into
every crevice of
emotional expression
fluidly experiencing
 it all
an overflow
of feminine knowing
of feminine feeling
I am but
a vessel for
 it all

  —luteal II

AHHHHHHHH

echoes into
the neverending
abyss
trailing off
to the edge
of space
ending nowhere
so loud
and everliving
it becomes
synonymous
with silence

just there

breathing it
      in
drowning in
      it
the waters
taking over me
spilling out
of my eyes
uncontrollably
I sob
   I heave
      I shake
trying to
be free of it
trying to
wring it
from my being

—luteal III

normalize
screaming
grunting
howling
at the Moon

normalize
vocally
expressing
anger
releasing through
and out
the body
into the ethers

liberated and
validated energy

now that the fury
has subsided
and Kali has returned
into Durga's third eye

here I am now
caught in the
downpour of
heart rain
feeling every beat
against my chest
feeling every tear
against my cheek

trying to
make sense
in the aftermath
of the storm
the chaos and
the destruction
that needed to
be done

in service
of my highest
good
lies the
disembodiment
of connections
that attempted to
siphon my energy
now severed
at the heads
destroyed

I lay down
my armor
and coddle

my heart

here I am now
caught in the
downpour of
heart rain
feeling every beat
against my chest
feeling every tear
against my cheek

now that the fury
has subsided
and Kali has returned
into Durga's third eye

feeling the weight
of my womb
filled with blood
brimming with decaying life
ready to be released
my heart in tandem
heavy
     heavy
         heavy
holding the weight
of loss   of grief
of anger   of betrayal
of holding onto
something that's
already gone

feeling the dissonance
in my own body
the offering is here
right on the edge
right on the brink
there is nothing
for me to do
but surrender into

     —PMF (premenstrual feelings)

tender
to the
touch
feeling
it all
the soreness
the softness
the spectrum
of being alive

my heart
is breaking
open

I am
surrendering
to it all
    the fear
    the desire
    the love
    the joy
    the pain
all is real

and so I feel
      I feel
          f e e l
              f
              e
              e
              l
        f
          e
            e
            l

until I am
but just
a feeling
buzzing
an energy
in motion

it's just below
the surface
of my skin
welling just
below my
tear ducts
sitting just
below my
voice box
a scream
a sob
an energy
on the
brink of
release

tears form
warm lakes
under my eyes
as they stream
down my face
I am cleansed
with waves
of relief
emotions
released
back into
the ocean
of existence

—cry II

there is no better place
to be than here
my womb and vulva
preparing for the levees
to break
blood shed
with reverence
my feet grounded
on the Earth
birds performing
a ceremonial song
she will bleed
and it will be
glorious

—personal red tent

I smell
the blood
the essence
of another cycle
gone past
of an unoccupied
womb
preparing
to shed

I smell
the blood
waiting at
the gates
of my vulva
like water
pressed against
a dam
ready to flood
open

I smell
the blood
the magic and
the medicine
inside my
womb

    —menstruation

woke up to
a flow of
     blood
     emotions
     water

running
   through me
     breaking
       from me

    —moontime arrives

when I bleed
silence is the only
thing that feeds me
running yolks
          break free
    spilling   every
which   direction
the consequences
of an egg unfertilized
a mourning commences
a celebration of a
previous life lived

    —the great release

time passes and I am still here

reflecting on
the intersectionality
of it all
the duality
the both-and

how can I connect without collapsing into
another completely?
how can I exist in this epic saga without
getting lost in the stories?
how can I trust with feet fully rooted in the
now without forcing my hand?
how can I be fully present

immersed
and engaged
and ready to let go at any moment?

can I free myself from the prisons of my stories
frozen in time?

can I stop projecting the past onto the present?
can I wipe the slate clean?
can I exist in the field of pure love and possibility?

can I be free from the time that no longer exists?

can I be free?
can I be free?
can I be free?

I attempt to
imitate an ideal
of perfection
as I've done
for decades

but the well
is running dry
and the excuses
that once filled it
are barren

and it gets
harder to try
and gather
a reason to be
anything but
this expression
that pulsates
so naturally
and vividly
from my being

changing shape
changing state
sometimes going
every which way
and sometimes
nowhere at all

sometimes
I have no control
over what seems
to arise out of me
and sometimes
I am perfectly aware

I attempt to

imitate an ideal
of perfection
but this is me
an   uncontrollable
        unpredictable
        wise and wild
        holy being

fate
cannot be
escaped
the tower
must crumble
so that
renewal
can occur
the wildness of
a pure heart
cannot be
controlled
the power
of love
cannot be
contained

there is no
escaping the
unfolding
it is already
happening

dimensions expanding
upon dimensions
timelines shifting
upon timelines

spiraling higher
grounding deeper
shedding faster
every time

surrendering and
releasing
releasing and
    surrendering

until I am naked
turned down to
bone   breath
and   blood

I have retreated
completely
like an orchid
entering her
resting period
before her eventual
rebloom

—menstruation II

all the beliefs
that were
never mine
are folding in
on themselves
houses made
of cards

I am here
face to face
with no one
but myself

my fears
and wounds
staring back
at me
seated patiently

a reflection
with no
agenda
just existence
calling
for integration

it's not about
anyone out there
it never is

     —ego death on repeat

cycling through
my psyche
lap after lap
no corner
left unsearched
like a scavenger
searching for
gold

I know the
expedition
will be worth
the trouble
and the journey
to the treasure
is only half
the battle of
retrieving myself

meeting exiled shadows
alchemizing and
integrating them
into the wholeness
of my being

traversing my own
ancient wounds
roots extending across
generations like a
mycelium network
of pain and trauma

rewiring neural pathways
reprogramming new beliefs
until me and everyone
connected to me
is free

tears cascade
from my eyes
like rivers
the rapid waters
become explosions
incinerating
any blockages
that stand
lodged
in the way
of my freest
flow

—cry III

the snake
rises in
the dark
like the kundalini
awakening
to its shakti

nothing
makes sense
when you are
submerged
in the infinite
darkness of
the void

it seems
like you are
    looping
stuck on
    repeat
spiraling

you wander
through
the darkness
for what feels
like eternity

eons pass by
and you are
still here
disoriented and
restless
held by
the vastness
and nurtured by
the unknown

you have
made it
your home
and just as
you begin
to find shelter
in the darkness
the light
begins to peak
plump and bright

finally
you can see
you realize
all you thought
had been stagnant
has morphed
including yourself
alchemy
has occurred
lead to gold

third eye
opens wide
as my cervix
follows suit
my womb
shedding
drop after
drop of blood
old life
seeking an escape
layers of tissue
thick with memories
the release overdue

third eye
seeing it all
so clearly
holding space
for understanding
beyond all reason
there is no hiding
from the
all-knowing
only truth
survives

—moontime vision

come
give me
your hand
beckons my
higher self

come
you are
ready

come
it is
time

I stand
with tears
in my eyes
knowing if
and when
I take her hand
the old timeline
will collapse
on itself
the old me
ceasing to
exist

I stand
with waves
of fear
radiating
through me
can I do this
I question
and just as quickly
as the question
arises
so does the

answer

yes
I can
I've done it
before and
I will do it
again

transcend
alchemize
this is nothing
new
stay open
breathe
step forward

come
give me
your hand
beckons my
higher self

come
you are
ready

come
it is
time

                —ascension

alarms ringing
turn into harmonies
and melodies that
build on one another
forming a bridge
to another perspective

—nervous system regulation

attempting
to live
life through
the heart

feeling the weight
and the power
the intention
holds
the portals
it opens
the accountability
it yields

to create
our reality
through simply
having the
audacity
to live
from our
truth

dropping into my body
letting it lead the way
has been Earth shattering
my internal compass
completely rewired
and reprogrammed
to honor
the feelings stemming
from my bones
the messages fluttering
from my nervous system
the whispers echoing
from my womb
the nudges sprouting
from my heart

red river
flowing out
of me
through
my womb
parted by the
sea of my lips
summoned by
the fullness
of the Moon

red river
like fire
burns through
all that needs
to be destroyed
with no mercy
just devotion
to return it
all to the
cosmic ocean

—moontime

I am falling in love
with every woman
who has had
the courage
to pry the skin
from her ribs
revealing
her heart
for the world
to see
the bravery
in standing tall
and bare
so sure
of oneself
in a world
that questions
everything about you

birthers of nations
this is the power
of the women
we know and
for whom we become

I know
I am
a living
breathing
angel
on Earth
a goddess
on land
   and I will not
   squeeze myself
   down out of
   the essence
   of my truth
   for you

  —honor me all

it is
safe

to trust
myself
above all
else

it is
safe

to trust
what I feel
sense and
know

deep in
my bones

I am coming
into form
after months of
what seemed like
never-ending
agony
breaking down
releasing
by choice
and by force
months of
mourning
grieving
struggling
to make peace
with the moment

suddenly
and yet
with time

I arrived at
a state of
inner peace
that could only
be cultivated
through witnessing
chaos and still
finding your way
to the center
to the eye
to the I
to the I am
presence
within you
that knows
all is well
at all times

that knows
a knowing
beyond time
and space

and through
this space
suddenly
something is
born

I feel her
energy pulsating
in rhythm with mine
her head peaking
out of the cervix
of my heart
she is emerging

    —another rebirth

dancing with
my shadow
in the heat
of the night
feeling
    the intimacy
    the tension
    the familiarity
as we breathe
neck in neck
chest to chest
for hours

until we lose
sense of who
is who
and where
one stops
and another
begins

until finally
we merge
union
occurs
we are
whole
once again

the forest burns
seemingly destroyed
only for it to
thrive again
        lush
           orgasmic
brimming with life

nothing exists
without purpose
nothing happens
without consequence

shedding and blooming
        shedding then blooming
        blooming and shedding
blooming then shedding

the cycle
        that never ends
    it intertwines
    until it is one
    yin and yang
    two parts
    consisting of
    the other
    completing
    one another
    two parts
    of the same
    oneness

the entirety
of the experience
is needed
to be whole

these years
have been
a consistent
death
          rebirth
a humble surrender

like a newborn
pushing through
the portal of the yoni
out of the darkness
into the light
bleeding beyond
the boundaries
of what once
contained me

I have been reborn
again and
          again and
again

I arrive at
the doorstep
of another level
 of devotion
 of surrender
 of embodiment

I arrive here
hopeful
disheveled
open and
ready

my heart is
overflowing
with a lifetime
of longing
 for the listening
 for the allowing
 for the acceptance
and adoration
of myself

it is time
to be
my greatest
beloved
in the way
that only
one can be
to oneself

knowing every
shadow and
secret

knowing every
wish and

desire

that constitute
my being

I arrive
at the doorstep
of my own heart
ready for sacred
union within

I have
stopped
seeking
I have
stopped
looking

for a love
that is said
to only live
outside of me

I have
become
my own
beloved
the great love
of my life

my inner warrior
a paradigm shattering
force propelled
by insurmountable
courage and
immovable conviction
external influences
stand no chance
for powers yield
to her
her word is bond
her action is inevitable
her intention is law
and all follows suit

blood
dripping from
my womb
month
after
month
an offering
to the Earth

sexual
sensual
erotic
energy
orgasmic
existence
a pleasure
tantra personified

wild
uncontrollable
undomesticated
running naked
with the wolves
howling at the
fullness
of the Moon

   —primal

serpent wisdom
the wild woman
is awakened
she pries
her way
out of the
paradise of
a prison
Eden will
never be
her home
she will not
be held captive
she will not
be suppressed
her body is
not a land
for conquest

the fire burns
from within
like Vesta
the hearth
is at my heart
and the river
is at my womb
the Moon inducing
the tides of my prana
and the summoning
of my blood
I am a wild woman
a creation
of the cosmos
a daughter
of the Earth
bone and blood

the phoenix rises
from the
ashes
pushed
through
the portal of
transmutation

this is the promise
of rebirth
a surrender
to descent
so that you
may one day
rise again

as my throat chakra
is cleared
broken through
and broken free

I feel the force
of sovereignty
before me
ancestors
past lives
past me's
the strength
of our voices
vibrating through
my being

their resilience
echoing in
my bones
the agony
of a truth
untold
and a truth
unlived
ringing through
my mind

reminding me
of the magnitude
of one's voice
and the power
of one's truth

allowing myself
to exist outside
of the lines
drawn by
our forefathers
remembering that
they too
can be erased

allowing myself
to remember
that limits
are only as real
as I make them
and removing
my confidence
dissolves them
back to the no-thingness
from which they came

I am reemerging
from my chrysalis
slowly unfurling
softening to the opening
of freedom
ready to
spread my wings
and fly

I am unstoppable
there is no mountain
too high

—follicular

I stand in the opaque darkness feeling the winds filled with desert dreams whisk past me.

behind me, I hear memories from moments passed all scattered behind doors that lead to halls that lead to nowhere. there is no going back. that is clear.

a part of me feels overcome with fear—I have transcended the past. a part of me feels unstoppable—I have transcended the past.

and in these past few years, I have died thousands of times, all in different ways. I have gone to the deepest and darkest parts of my being and come back with a boundless light.

and here I stand almost totally disconnected from the past. standing at the gateway of a new life.

from the seed
I was planted
to be
deep in the weeds
fighting for light
to beam
space
to bloom

to the flower
I am blossoming
to become
rooted deeply
budding strongly
bearing fruit
fragrant and
sweet

a fire is blazing
in the chambers
of my heart
that refuses
to be diffused
it is eternal and
it is raging
and I have decided
to let it consume me

the empress
magnetic and
alluring
like a flower
blossomed and
full of pollen
buzzing with
potential

I am in
full bloom
a sight to see
radiating and
brimming
with nectar
ready to relish
life itself

—ovulation

chapter two

echoes of the earth

I arrive at
the oak tree
with the branches
that chose to
kiss the Earth

the river
with the stones
that only show
when it's wishing
for rain
just ahead
of me

it all seems
familiar like
déjà vu
a memory
from a
different me
that's lived
this moment
times before

the sound of
leaves falling
away
a trigger
of feelings
of decays
and rebirths
that have
taken place
in this clay
of a body

as I sit
on the banks
of the river
I feel as
though I am
      the wind
      the water
      the stranger
across the way
observing it all

the boundaries
disappear
back into
the mirage
nothing
is separate
submerged
into the
piscean waters
the boundless
ocean of
the cosmos
and Gaia
and everything
in between

crying
to the river
finding solace
and support
as she shows me
that it is okay
to be
overflowing
with emotion

screaming
to the wind
out goes all the
           anguish
           and anger
it is allowed to exist
outside of me
to be carried
beyond me
off to another place
for it to be free
of the constraints
of my human body
for me to be free
of the type of tension
that only comes
from the pressure
of suppression

laying
on the Earth
feeling my heart
beat in tandem
with the Mother
pulse by pulse
current by current

watching the trees sway
as the Sun finds its way
through the
dense crown

    its light
            breaking through
the gaps
reaching the
ground below

showing me
subliminally
light will always
    find its way
         to you
no matter
how deep
in the shadows
you believe yourself
to be

the buds wilt
preparing
for the petals
to fall
like
my heart
preparing
for the grudges
to follow suit
for the pain
to be freed
for the hurt
to rot back
into the Earth

electro
    magnetic
s h i f t s

in the Earth's
core
echo into
mine

I am rocked
from my center
equilibrium
         disjointed
recalibration
is necessary
reset unavoidable

    I remain still
    suspended
    in between
until
a reconnection
occurs
a new path
is illuminated
a new ground
is found

    —when the Earth quakes

rolling tides
form mountains
and valleys
the Earth meets
the sea

erosion is inevitable
the tower must
crumble
and I will not
resist the landslide
of release

I grant it permission
to compost that which
no longer sustains me

I grant it permission
to sprout passions
madly like wildflowers
which know no bounds
upon the endless plains

I grant it permission
to debunk and deconstruct
all falsehoods
so that only
the truth of life
may shine through
like the boundless Sun

amidst the wind
and the trees

I am able
to access the
universal intelligence
inside of me
a portal opens
and I slip inside
like Alice in
her wonderland
all is alive
and seemingly
existing outside
of time

amidst the wind
and the trees

I lose myself
completely
I find myself
in every beetle
and rock
I am no longer
separate
I extend
every which
way
I am it all
I am whole
and complete

I awaken
inside the heart
of the Earth
buried to
be reborn
the baptism
of dirt
rinsing me
clean
absorbing
the density
from my being

I awaken
inside the heart
of the Earth
to the beating
of drums
echoing
from my chest
sending vibrations
of home out
to all the rest
of the galaxy

I awaken
inside the heart
of the Earth
feeling like
a newborn
in the womb
safe
awaiting
my transition
through the portal
of the yoni
of Gaia
back to land

it is safe
for me to
be here now
eyes wide open
feet planted
firmly
on the ground
rooted
heart to heart
with Gaia
held
by the love
that only
a mother
could give

in nature
I cease
to exist

ego dissolves
carried off
into the wind

karma is
swallowed whole
by the Earth

psychological walls
are washed away
by the river

through the light
of the Sun
I become love

levitating upon
the Earth
her torus field
infused with
intergalactic wisdom

miracles await
in the bountiful
offerings
that erupt
from her fertile soil

insights
beaming down
like a sunshower
gentle and nourishing
the medicine
is rooted
in the magic
of the dirt

there is
a time for harvesting
a time for seeding
a time for pruning
a time for weeding

in the present
open and ready
never rushing
never hesitating
always knowing
inspired action
divine unfolding
timing always perfect

—garden lessons

the land
holds medicine
healing that goes
beyond skin
and bones
straight to the seat
            of the soul

            —Earth medicine

belly to Earth
the idea of
who we've been
    shifting
beneath us

our skin
ripping   at
the   seam
like the
caterpillar
dissolving
into no-thing

evolution is
the only choice
transformation
the natural law

      —serpent medicine

going deep
connecting
with the wisdom
of the trees
divine intelligence
stretching wide
and far
beyond
the constructs
of time
going back
centuries
to the seed
of humanity

bathing in
the light
of the Sun
its fire
activating me
with light codes
higher realms
higher frequencies
higher ways
of being

crystallizing
grounding
connecting
with nature
an extension
of my
human body
earth
water
air and
fire

enveloped
in the magic
of being alive
here on Earth

of being able
to hear
the blue jay sing
joyous symphonies

of being able
to feel
the dewy soil
resting beneath
my feet

of being able
to smell
the sea air
crisp with salt

of being able
to see
the Sun bursting
with an array of colors
like the star it is

clouds drift by
do they
       ever arrive
           in the same
           state
       in which
they set off?

shape   shifting
           morphing
           transforming
by the second

we drift by
       where are
       we going?
do we
       ever arrive
           in the same
           state
       in which
we set off?

shape   shifting
           morphing
           transforming
by the second

the ever-changing
landscape of Gaia
exists within
each of us

the plethora
of   shapes
          textures
          smells
          tones and
          temperatures
that make up
the uniqueness
of each environment
can be found
on the plains
of our bodies

our existence
consisting of
tropical lush
rainforests
barren deserts
steep clear
mountaintops
wide open fields
expansive waters
and everything
in between

I awaken
to the pitter-patter
of rain drops
softly falling
on the shingles
of the roof

my heart
beating in unison

my emotions
like the rain drops
full
       gentle
and
       bursting

the sky
gloomy
and gray
like the space
in between
my thoughts
unclear and
all-encompassing

I find peace
here
in my body
against
the warmth
of the sheets

in the solidness
and the transience
of this moment

—Sunday morning storm

the rain
repeatedly
kisses
the Earth
drop
after
drop
it surrenders
its unwavering
never-ending
devotion
to the
nourishment
of Pachamama

the Sun
is shining and
rain is falling

a baptism
an initiation
a witch is
getting married

a divine union
the high priestess
has found her priest

a miracle
that all the elements
eagerly desire
to bear witness to
a fairy tale
come true

      —sunshowers

Persephone
has returned
from the
underworld
and she is
bearing fruit

—spring equinox

I rise
in the rainforest

to the orchestra
of a thousand birds

to the echoing chorus
of howling monkeys

singing
in unison

rise

rise
like the dense fog
from the valleys
of the mountains

rise
like the Sun
from below the horizon
glimmering upon the ocean

rise

connecting with
the wisdom
bathing in
the light
new life codes
ancient truths
coming online

connecting with
the wisdom
bathing in
the light
gaining new sight
my senses rebooted
with new life

—sunbathing

her rays of light
illuminating
every low
dense energy
that attempts
to hide
in the darkness
to cling
to the shadows

her rays of light
touching
everything
in sight
blessing it
with the expansion
of new life

her rays of light
awakening
to higher
dimensions
where the beloved
is everywhere
and love
is the only
truth

—she's like the Sun

water your garden
tend to your fire
be the object
of your own desire

you are a rose
thorns protruding
sharply
        petals budding
        softly
the feminine
        and the
        masculine
divine sacred union
embodied within
expression and
protection
love and honor
        coexisting
        coinhabiting
        one being

sipping from
the infinite nectar
of your own heart
you've found
an eternal bliss

—hummingbird medicine

the wild woman
one with
the rhythms
of the drums
that resemble
the beat
of her heart
that mimic
her footsteps
as they kiss
the ground
of the Earth
in sync

they say
she is here

her cycles
in tune
with the Moon
both reaching
their peak
both ready
to flow
to bleed
to birth
new stars
like the oracle
that she is

like a tree
I allow all
the branches
of me
to roam free

every branch
a part
of the sum
of who I am
in totality

the hermetic alchemist
the multidimensional creatrix
the phoenix child
the venusian lover
the wild wise woman
the parts of me
undiscovered and
uncontainable

all these parts
branching off
into their own
galaxy
yet stemming
from the same
rooted trunk
the same
boundless source

blazing forth
a spark
turned wildfire
chaotic and
life-giving
containing and
transcending
duality
both primal
and sophisticated
destroyer and
creator
no stranger
to birth
nor death
every part
used for the
resurrection
the phoenix
burns again

—fire medicine

do not
walk this Earth
afraid
for you
are one
with the 5D
crystalline grid
every mycelium
thread
weaving
its way
beneath you
a network
of support

head to the ground
I bow
crown to crown
root to root

body and Earth
tree of life
mirrored
connected

one unified energy
torus fields feeding
into one another
infinitely

cycling
figure eights
encircling
abundantly

soul star
to Earth star
feet to the ground
tethered

I hear
the Earth speak
to me in whispers
so gentle they
echo through
my being
in frequencies

reminding me
of my innate
primal state
a wild woman
undomesticated
and in harmony
with the natural
rhythms of
the Earth

reminding me
I am nature
in all of her
calm and chaos
in all of her
darkness and light

reminding me
she is my home
where all of
me is welcome
and all of
me is seen
because all of
me is her
an echoed
existence

skin brown
like the soil
receptive to the
rays of the Sun
heart absorbing
all the light
the leaves
cannot take

I am but
another bloom
an offspring
of the Earth

lotus flower
in the garden
gracefully
birthing beauty
from the darkness

lotus flower
in the garden
growing soft
when you should've
been hardened

lotus flower
in the garden
blooming bright
with a
resilient light

flowing
    and morphing
        through dimensions
of existence

what is realer
than what
you feel
to be true?

knowing
the truth is
an ever-changing
state like you

      —water medicine

rain turns
to the river
     to feel
         whole again

I turn
to the river
     to feel
         love again

we are
the same
the rain
and I

dripping ourselves
     moment by moment
back into the river
     with devotion

the river
snakes her
life force
kundalini
through the
terrain
up the
spine of
Mother Earth
birthing
new life
with every
notch
she turns

the tree
digs her
roots deep
lifetime after
lifetime
through the
vital land
down the
spine of
Mother Earth
until all
is connected
one mass
organism

water. our first mother. holding us bare and naked in the womb. now, in the rivers and oceans, Oshun and Yemaya cradling us. the all and the no-thing. the full creative potential and the void. the limitless unconscious turned conscious, visible, and tangible. the calm and the storm. the life and the death. water.

my womb
is like the ocean
the all-encompassing
no-thing
birthed into form
containing multitudes
of waves
feeling everything
alchemizing
through salt
and water

holding all possibilities
to the sustenance
of life
while simultaneously
holding the power
to destroy
and deconstruct
until nothing
remains
in the darkness
but mystery

waters choppy
and serene
still yet
flowing
constantly
unfolding upon
itself
like the
thousand-petal
lotus flower
self-realized

the sea feels
like home

a comfort
long known
an embrace
long felt
that lives
in the ligaments
of my muscles
and in the crevices
of my mind

the sea feels
like home

a feeling
not new
a language
unknown
strange yet
familiar
distant yet
safe
like a galaxy
from which
I came

the sea feels
like home

the harmony
of the waves
the ultimate
sound bath

attuning all
my chakras

purifying
my meridians

cleansing
my energy

immersed
in natures
432 hertz

like the oyster
my soul
transformed
the parasites
to something
beautiful and
timeless

layer after
layer
time passing
time
until a pearl
was made
precious and
iridescent

ready to reflect
the light
to feel
the softness
and the joys
of being open
once again

the mountain peak
this is why
we're here
to feel alive

life is bursting
out the seams
an orgasmic
overflow

the great expansion
days abundant
with illumination
ripe for savoring

—summer solstice

in the heart
of the Sun
we become
love
potent and
bold

—cazimi

the sunlight
dances upon
the leaves
like ballerinas
prancing about
a mahogany stage

water trickling
across the river stones
like tap dancers
scatting seamlessly
into harmonies and
melodies

dragonflies
blue and black
spinning in circles
like the Sufis
enlightened
and drunk on God

memories scattered
on every block
like streetlights

love grows here
like weeds
invasive but
it knows
no bounds

pain and trauma
composted
into fertilizer
for the harvest
of transgenerational
healing

a new story
was written
glory
    glory
        glory
a new story
was written

        —hometown/Orlando

mystical and
magical peninsula
tropical swampland
enchanted with
Spanish moss
curtained from trees
as far as
the eyes
can see
from sea to
shining sea

—Flor(ida) II

summer rays and
summer rains
remind me
of a time
when the only
abundance
was laughter
tan lines
flip cups and
curfews missed

when staying out
until the streetlights
came on was like
being rewarded
a spotlight for a
day well lived

when tomorrow
was just another day
for the adventure
to continue
best friends   crushes
sleepovers   meetups
at the green box
bikes scattered across
the lawn like constellations
across a night sky
promising we'll
meet again tonight

—childhood summers

the sunshine meets me
joyously each morning like
stars meet me at night

—haiku

drifting
there are no
            directions
      when   everywhere
e x i s t s

who needs
      an anchor
when you have   wings to fly?

            —air medicine

hop on a plane
and cross
the borders of
your own mind
to perspectives
uncharted

like psychedelics
melting
the boundaries of
your reality
new perceptions
are awakened
your consciousness
forever altered
expanded by
the potency of
your experiences

—travel

rainy days in Nola remind me of rainy days in Santa Tere. seeking refuge in cafes with sweet treats and warm drinks. snuggled amongst strangers and friends and those with whom the line seems to blur. hand to pen, spilling out every thought onto the paper that is porous and open. eager and ready to merge with every word. nose to book, eyes losing themselves into another reality completely, body still seated here. present and connected. rainy days in Nola remind me of rainy days in Santa Tere.

every second beamed with opportunity, with perfection. the rain, the dust, the smiles of strangers who became friends before they became strangers again.

—Santa Tere

the city lights
glittered
amongst
the mountains
like a million
fireflies dancing
on the face
of the Earth
welcoming me
with glee

—Medellin

the sisterhood
of the traveling stars
legends who shine
brighter than
the Sun

—Pleiades

lions
Auset and
Egyptian
pyramids

Lemuria
Atlantis and
the Dogon
too

the stargate
to higher frequencies
and unity
anchoring light codes
of possibilities
to our galaxy

    —Sirius

high off the moonlight
my feet move
uncontrollably
to the beat
my arms flow
to the harmony

high off the moonlight
I daydream
of kissing you
I laugh
at the undeniable
truth of it all

high off the moonlight
I become liberated
able to be
        free
        true
        pure
expression

high off the moonlight
reflecting the light
of the Sun

      —full Moon

the wild woman
howling at the
plumpness of
the Moon

Lilith running
naked with
the wolves
uninhibited and free

I was born
on a waxing
gibbous Moon
growing towards
fulfillment

always aiming
for the fullness
of the light

feeling the call
to keep
illuminating
expanding
to wholeness

as the Moon
finds its fullness
nestled on the
edge of infinity

the tides of
my life turn in
sacred rhythm

the seeds explode
from the soil
like shooting stars

the harvest
is ready
plump and ripe

the light of
the Sun
shines from
my heart

meet me under
the moonlight
where we
become starlight
where we
merge back
into no-thing
into one

meet me under
the moonlight
where our
imperfections melt
into the shadows
of the night
and the truth
of our energy
is the only
illumination

yellow flower
in the meadow
shining bright
even in
the height
of the night
like the Sun
under the light
of a thousand stars

—evening primrose

fields of wildflowers
the smell of honeydew
a free spirit frolicking
amongst the birds
and the bees
dancing with the wind
all seems at peace

when suddenly
the Sun disappears
shadowed by
the darkness
of storm clouds
Oya is amongst us
trees rustle
chattering of
the change to come

hoping I can bend
like them
praying I can stay
rooted
and not break
hoping I don't get
carried away

the bamboo
is strong
and it is solid
but it is hollow

empty and
ready to
bend
any which
way
allowing
the current
of life
to mold it
resisting nothing

empty and
ready to
be moved
by the cosmic
force
of the now
never holding
onto anything
yet purposefully
rooted in itself

as the light
finds its way
back to
the darkness
and yang
turns yin
we find the
perfect harmony
the balance
of it all
the fall after
the rise
greens turn
to browns
and the
harvest awaits
to be reaped
the descent
begins soon

—fall equinox

the flowers
are falling
from the trees
a living example
that blooming
must cease
some day
the pungent
fragrance
cannot be
sustained
forever

the flowers
are falling
from the trees
like bleeding
hearts
inviting us
to feel
beyond
what we see
to become
more than
we perceive

leaves of reds
        browns
        and oranges
pepper the ground
like snowflakes
unique and
transient

a layer of
decay
blankets the sidewalks
a constant reminder
of change
at every
step

you can
love something
with every
molecule
in your being
and still know
deep within
your soul
that it is time
to let it
go

—plant medicine doesn't only come
from psychedelics

the leaves fall
one by one
reaching towards
the river
a never-ending
shower of kisses
welcoming themselves
back into the current
of life

what was once
separate
becomes one
again

let go
with grace
there is nothing
to hold onto
bareness is
fruitful too

—tree wisdom

shifting
          changing
quickly
like the wind
switches direction
amidst
a coming storm

shifting
          changing
quickly
like tectonic plates
startled by
the sudden rush
of friction

shifting
          changing
quickly
like a current
changes pace
upon
a rising tide

shifting
          changing
quickly
like a cloud
finding its form
indefinitely morphing
neither solid
nor spirit
drifting
          somewhere in
          between

the pinnacle
of darkness
silent
and somber
there is
nowhere
to go
but inward
all else
has contracted
in on itself
a retreat
for rejuvenation
there is medicine
in the stillness
there is life
in the void

—winter solstice

walking into
the pitch-black
darkness
of the night
with only stars
in sight
ready
and willing
to face
whatever
should arise
trusting in
my knowing
instinctive
and intuitive
trusting in
my power
feminine
and fierce

—jaguar medicine

the surface
is bare
seemingly
lifeless

and yet

below
there is
nothing
but life

fungi and
earthworms
thriving beneath
the soil
rich and vibrant
fertile and ready
the foundation
tending to itself
preparing
the conditions
for future creations
to effortlessly
mature

the surface
is bare
seemingly
lifeless

and yet

just like all
in this
earthly reality
which transcends
logic and labels

two seemingly
opposite realities
are existing
as one

two seemingly
opposite truths
are existing
at once

the sky is a quilt
patches of gray
turned muted blue
gloom turned glimmer
seen through
the right eyes

new Moon
blank space
fertile yet void

the contradictions
of the feminine
all birthed forth
from the womb
of the mother
who birthed it all

the chaos
and the order
the no-thing
and the all

new Moon
feminine waters
the wave and
the ocean

Yemaya calls
you deep
can you release
your anchor
so you can drift
can you get out
of your shell
so you can grow
and occupy
a space so vast
that the only way
to fill it
is to become
the void itself
forever expanding
free from constraints

from the trees
I learn to
surrender
to the wisdom
of time
in all of
its scales
seconds to centuries
and every increment
in between
meaningful and
imbued with
purpose

from the trees
I learn there
is nothing
more beautiful
than being
and allowing
every cycle
and expression
with grace
every wilt
and crooked branch
every sprout
that goes nowhere
every branch that
extends every
which way

from the trees
I learn to
honor the
sacredness
and perfection
of the process
the brittle death

the silence and
the emptiness
that seems
endless
days of what
feel like
eternal darkness
where we are
nothing but seeds
stored in the
depths of the soil
an eternity
passes by
and the cycle
begins again

the Big Bang
the ecstatic
orgasm that
never ends
only builds
on itself
release
after release
higher and
higher
until it
crescendos
and life
is born
spring is
here

the past is buried

back into the Earth
composted and
unrecognizable

absorbed
back into the void
of the great womb

back to the
Great Mother
to become new life

layer after
layer
of wilted petals

pile after
pile
of dead roots

removed
until I was
free of debris
able to bloom
in full

    —flower essences

soaring above
the land
a new vision
is found
your perspective
your new superpower

—eagle medicine

shooting stars
grace the stage
of the glittering
night sky
leaving behind
trails of gold

blades of grass
dance in the wind
swaying with
the currents
pulsating with love

clouds of dreams
swirl across
the ocean sky
spelling out hellos

I become one
with it all
effortlessly
melting into
the landscape
of existence

—all is alive/mushroom medicine

the Earth is conscious
alive and breathing

connected to
all which she births
in tune with
all parts of herself

the waters
her blood
the lands
her bones

confined to
this atmosphere
yet boundless in
her forms

like a mother
with unconditional
love for herself
knowing nothing fruitful
comes from being
a martyr

and healthy love
is rooted in boundaries
reciprocity and honoring
oneself and the other

the Earth is conscious
and she is speaking
demanding her respect

praying for
the veil
of ignorance
to be lifted
from our eyes
so we may
stop killing
each other

blood spilled
so egos can
survive and
economies
can thrive
what a
shallow
sacrifice

—there's more to life on Earth

the Earth has
borne witness to
many unnecessary sacrifices
the blood spilled
unwarranted and unneeded

may the blood
from our moons
offered up in love
balance the karma
of human violence

may we return
home to the
Great Mother Earth
asking for mercy
and forgiveness
for our grand
grievances
bowing and
communing
with her
in great reverence
like our ancestors
who knew
they were nothing
without her

the vulvas
of the Earth
dark   moist
and   full of
ancient wisdom
revered by groups
of antiquity
for her mysteries

whispering of a
simpler time
when human
and Earth
were one

      —caves

we as humans
are not the rulers
of this planet
we are merely
visitors in this
blip of time

and what will withstand
as it always has
are the mountains
the deserts
the oceans
and the lands
in between

can we learn
from mycelium
like a mentee
learning from
a sage
the true meaning
of community
beyond survival
of the individual

sharing resources
and protecting
one another
choosing collaboration
so that the whole
can thrive

seeds and roots
the future and
the past intertwine

the roots
go deep
retracing
our connection
through the dawn
of time
through the center
of the Earth
back to
the garden of Eden
where Lilith
tends to the potential
of us all

seeds and roots
the future and
the past intertwine

the seeds
spread far
riding the waves
of the wind
to distant lands
that whisper promises
of continued
regeneration
for generations
to come
filled with the
enchanting possibilities
of new beginnings
and legacies
fulfilled

boundless
blue ocean
boundless
blue sky
we are
the same
you
and
I

stretching out
infinitely
towards
depths
unknown
and
heights
unfathomed
yet seen as one
dimensional
blue
despite
containing a
multitude
of hues

boundless
blue ocean
boundless
blue sky
we are
the same
you
and
I

existing beyond
labels

existing beyond
whys

we are all
finding our own
path toward
the light
bending
sprouting
in the uniqueness
of freedom

there is nothing
to compare
no consistency
in snowflake
to snowflake
Uranus to
Venus
souls taking on
many forms
shapeshifting
through eons
of timelines
every role
perfect

sweet grass
sweet water
sweet smoke
sweet daughter

of the mother
in the belly
of the caves
in the breasts
of the mountaintops
and the blood
of the rivers
a sacred extension
of Gaia
interconnected
overlapping until
we become
one entity
in harmony
our existence
medicinal

waves of water
waves of frequency
waves of you and me
becoming infinity

looping around
one another
endlessly
in the dance
of rasalila
heaven on
Earth

waves of water
waves of frequency
waves of you and me
existing infinitely

stretching far
forward
backward
outward
and inward
holding and
loving all life
the garden
of Eden
is here
the Earth
is heaven

we go in cycles
around the Sun
dancing in moons
on Earth
we wilt
    we die
        we are
                reborn

chapter three

dancing with the divine

I am
    collapsing
    in
on myself
yet again
    imploding
back to the
source
   fading
    to no-thing

while the magnificent
urge arises
within me
   to burst forth
    into a million galaxies
a trillion stars
shining bright
   spanning across
     light years
against the backdrop
of the womb
of the infinite mother

I am
   unfurling
   beyond
myself

I have been
submerged
back into
the vastness
of the darkness
temporarily losing
the sense of
who I am
is inevitable

who I am
is no longer
clear
merging back
with the mother

who I am
is scattered
amongst
the zero
point field

the concept
of me
now moving
points
nothing is
solid
I feel
disjointed
but I am
lighter

choices are
mine
how high
do I want
to fly

how deep
do I want
to dive

who do I
want to be
when I
reemerge
remembering
nothing is
solid
anything is
possible
all is moving
points
awaiting
      my alignment

learning to be empty
resisting the urge
to fill the space
to rush to meaning
to stretch so thin
that I am not whole

learning to be empty
without standing guard
at the doorway
of my own being
without clinging
to moments
that only exist
in the networks
of my mind

internally feeling
at the crossroads
again
but this time
making a different
choice

internally feeling
like I am emptying
and knowing
this is good

that in this
burning down
of the old
        new life
will sprout
that in this
stillness of no-thing
        the combustion
of something

will emerge

and yet
this emptying
petrifies me
as I am
called over
and over
and over
to surrender
to disappear
to not exist
as I once was

the fear begins
to consume me
I wonder
is this how
the caterpillar
felt before
it dissolved
into no-thing

if so
then I must
too have faith
that in this void
I shall become
far greater
than I could've
ever imagined

I don't know
   I don't know
      I don't know
         I don't know

I repeat
into the
crevices
of my mind

the words
echo and
reverberate
through
the vessels
that line
my bones

I don't know
   I don't know
      I don't know
         I don't know

the words
that once
paralyzed me
in fear and
saturated me
with unease

now feel
like the warm
embrace of
comfort

I don't know
   I don't know
      I don't know
         I don't know

for how
    could I
        possibly know

for how
    could I
        possibly know

for how
    could I
        possibly know

I am but
a speck

deeper into
the never-ending
spiral
feeling pushed
to the ends
scared to let go

where will
it take me

I am existing
in between
one reality
and the next
        constantly
it seems

        constantly
in flux
        constantly
between
one timeline
and the next
        constantly
standing at the
access point
to the zero
point field

        constantly
nowhere
and everywhere

yet   constantly
seeking
the comfort

of knowing

of stillness
of sameness

of movement
of newness
of surprises

my paradoxes
existing at once
the paradoxes
existing at once
the paradox
of it
all existing
at once

of no
true state
or structure
or solidity

       the wholeness
       the oneness
       so vast
       so multidimensional
that it seems
unable to grasp
always outside
of one's reach

yet
in the moment
of total
final surrender
you feel it all
       the wholeness
       the oneness
       the vastness

the multidimensionality
within yourself

that has no
true state
or structure
or solidity

constantly
in flux
constantly
between
one timeline
and the next
constantly
standing at the
access point
to the zero
point field

constantly
nowhere
and everywhere

allowing and
choosing
in every moment

deeper into
the never-ending
spiral
feeling pushed
to the ends
knowing there
is no end
scared to let go
scared to release
control

where will it
take me

I don't know
but still
I let go

  —constantly here and beyond

I surrender
I wave the
white flag
taking a
gracious bow

and then
in one
continuous
motion
I trust fall
from the deck
of the ship
into the currents
of life

I become
submerged
in the sense
of safety
you can only
feel in
the womb
of a mother

I surrender
completely
to the flow
knowing
these waves
are carrying
me with love

in the belly
of the mother
I am immersed
in her waters
reformed and
reborn
tethered from
womb to womb
the waves
of grace
wash over me
delicately

I am softened
my bones
become tender
and flexible
shapeshifting
seamlessly weaving
through fabrics
of existence
in the stillness
all is in motion
in the liminal
there is liberation

ultimate release
of control
drifting blindly
into the void
unable to sense
boundaries or
hints of form
Divine Mother
challenging me
to surrender
to a faith
beyond all
comprehension
to merge
so organically
with the flow
that I become
a mere grain
of sand
always on
the edge of
the no-thing and
the everything
where miracles
and magic
unfold

I am on
the ledge
looking over
into a sea
of darkness
that shimmers
with stars
that when I
gleam closer
unfold
into galaxies
of potentials
the slate
is blank
yet pulsing
with possibility

I am leaping
over this pit
of quicksand
that seems to
be made of
shards of glass
and broken
hopes

I am free falling
into the arms
of the Divine
Mother
trusting
and knowing
she will catch
me

there is no
controlling this
it is happening

the fault lines
that hold
all past truths
have cracked
open
and I
am okay
because I
have wings

I am flying
remembering
my power
activating
an innate
knowing

I am soaring
gliding effortlessly
with the mass
love energy
of the cosmos

I've come into the unknown, surrendered.
found my footing, while loosening my mind.
do you believe in portals? in gateways? in
these moments in the space-time continuum
that push us into another dimension within
and outside of ourselves? shifting the fabric
of our very beings, our known existence
reupholstered until we are completely
renewed.

I surrender to
the alchemical fire
time and
time again

all that is
not true
burns away
and returns
back to no-thing
a symbolic death
a sacred offering
for my desired
life to be birthed
from the ashes
of my last

I am reborn
transmutation
after transmutation
a phoenix
forever rising

magic in
the light

illumination
dancing upon
the dark

something sparks
consciousness
ignites

new life
is born

as I become
more empty
I become
more full

like the winds
of a hurricane
or the rampage
of a goddess
wild chaos
ensures
destruction
of the rotten
before
the bloom
of the fruit

on the red road

I travel
through spirit
and matter
north to south
honoring them
both the same

on the red road

I travel
through shadow
and light
east to west
honoring them
both the same

on the red road

I travel
down every path
finding truth
in every direction
honoring it
all the same

ping-pong across
the board of
consciousness

going from
the height
of the other
to the depth
of the self

and somehow
seeing
the middle path
the only path
the only experience
being perceived

one so vast
the only way
to digest the
multitude of it
is to create
categories
and boundaries

that only collapse
into one another
eventually
all to none
zero to one

the spiral of life
the ancient whirlpool
that sucks you in
down to the depths
of the ocean floor
surrounded by
darkness unexplored

then
you are lifted up
to the heavens
past all layers
of the stratosphere
until you can
kiss God

then
again
you nose-dive
back down
to the abyss
where you are
one with it all

around and through
cycle upon cycle
shedding
and embodying
death and
rebirth
this is the
natural flow

the helix of life
never ceasing
always swaying
to and fro
yet balanced
on a single
point

eternally here
the past
and the future
solely extensions
of our minds
an organ
encased
by flesh

our consciousness
connected to
a vast source
so indescribable
that even centuries
of gurus
saints
and oracles
detailing
is not enough
to satisfy
the yearning
soul

hungry for
a truth
beyond
what is given
because
what is true
cannot be known

only felt
through
experiencing

the great
        spiral
going up
        going down
deeper
        higher

while
simultaneously
going
no where

because
there is
nowhere
to go

all is here
        everything
everywhere
        all at once

in this
moment
timelines
unfold
the future
is now
all possibilities
are present

life is
a lucid dream
all more fluid
than it seems
disappearing
and reappearing
expanding and
contracting
in one
epic symphony

life is
a lucid dream
I am the
dreamer
and the
dream
the cosmic
seamstress
weaving her way
through the
multidimensionality

the indistinguishable illusion
the passionate play
the captivating comedy
the triumphant tragedy

—samsara

what if Kali
was in her rage
joyously?

dancing
the death
dance

slicing
the heads
of illusions

all with
ecstatic
bliss

death
anger
the dark side
of the mother
they say
as if it were
a stain upon
the purity of
the idea
they assumed
the feminine
to be

screams
earthquakes
aches
moans
cyclones
chaos ensues
it seems
like havoc
because it
cannot fit into
the confinements
of their
little box

laughter
rivers
orgasms
flowers blooming
crops maturing
bountiful
nurturing
love embodied
the light of
the Sun
that expands

beyond
their reach

the feminine
is all form
is all from
which life
springs forth
and all from
which life
will return

she is the
decay of
remains
she is the
blood that
drips forth
every month
from the womb
she is the
first breath
we take

the feminine
is the totality
of life itself

      the feminine
      is the totality
      of life itself

            the feminine
            is the totality
            of life itself

daughter of
the divine
birthed from
the womb
of the cosmic
mother
faceless
yet called
by many
names
there is no
mistaking
her presence
or her power
for she is
the one

I am
that
I am

no matter
what you
choose
to call me

—the goddess wears many names

the high priestess
the one who knows
the one who is
a channel
for the divine
and the divine
herself

Earth in my bones
stars in my lungs
exploding
into supernovas
galaxies birthing
within my womb

I am more
than your idea
of a woman
defined by
her body
existing in
the confines
of your limited
logic

I dance with
the divine
in dimensions
unseen
visiting parallel
realities
in my
dreams

time and space
are not constructs
to me
when consciousness
exists beyond
human need

my dreams
are portals
to other lands
and other realms

unforeseen
possibilities
and alternate
realities
unfolding
before me

my mind's eye
a multidimensional
transmitter of
guidance
inspiration and
subconscious
truths

all presented
before me
vividly

gateways to
dimensions unknown
yet familiar
to my soul

mirrors to
my mind
and portals
to my psyche

messengers
from the
higher realms
divine interventions

  —dreams

red Moon
full Moon
thirteenth passage
activated
ancient goddess
magic

red Moon
full Moon
thirteenth passage
dormant codes
awakened
priestess   seer
medicine   woman
creatrix   healer

red Moon
full Moon
thirteenth passage
initiated in my
thirteenth year
thirteen cycles
womb to Moon
blood to Earth
root to crown
kundalini uncoiled
the path of the
divine feminine
wide open

inside
every woman
exists three
cycling
her being
the holy
trinity

a maiden
curious
open and ready
to penetrate
her way
into the world
like a seedling
bursting forth
from its coat
into the warm
springtime air
filled with the
taste of adventure
and innocence
wild
free
and searching
for pleasure
in the hunt

a mother
abundant
secure and mature
ready to harvest
her sowing
under the light
of the full Moon
fertile and buzzing
with sexual
creative energy

like the height
of the summer
solstice
crowning and
open for birth

a crone
wise
resilient and
steeped
in the darkness
of the deep
mysteries
a kaleidoscope
of life's experiences
waning
like the Moon
back into
the canvas
of the cosmic
womb
the ending
the inevitable death
and the courage
it takes
to face it
with grace
surrendering
back into
the seed

inside
every woman
exists three
cycling
her being
the holy
trinity

medial woman
one foot in this
earthly realm
and the other
in spirit
lover of the
lobos and
the liminal
the multidimensional
messenger

I cannot
be defined
there are
no structures
that can create
perimeters
around the
boundlessness
of which I am

       I am not stationary
always fluidly
             moving
through the
       multidimensionality
of my soul's embodiment

I am constantly
discovering myself
in new ways
and old
unfolding like
the thousand-petal
lotus flower
in which
there is never
a point when
all is known

liberation
cannot exist
in the confines
of a cage

even if
the bars are
spread wide and
there are windows
and doors
it is still
a cage

and where
there are
barriers
there are
restrictions

and where
there are
restrictions
there is
oppression

and where
there is
oppression
there is
injustice

and where
there is
injustice
there is
never true
liberation

we are bone
and blood
animal and
Earth with a
boundless spirit
on a quest
of heroine's
to break free
from the mirage
that we are only
born to suffer
work and die

we are bone
and blood
animal and
Earth with a
boundless spirit
on a quest
of heroine's
destined for a
sovereign life
to experience the
miracle of heaven
on Earth

I resist like Auset
words in my mouth
ready to speak my
desires into being
resurrection is possible
and it lives on my tongue

I resist like Kali Ma
blade in hand
slicing off the heads
of all who dare
attempt to destroy
the highest order

I resist like Quan Yin
compassion blooming
from my heart like
the thousand-petal
lotus flower
my love knowing
no bounds

I resist like Oshun
joy emanating
from my being
hips swinging to
the rhythm of life
in love with existence
my energy the source
of creation itself

the revolution
cannot be contained
because it has already
grown wild roots

making its home
across cultures
and oceans
in places unseen

expanding with
every breath
the collective takes in
the pursuit of freedom

smile as a
protest
laugh as a
revolution
play as a
political
statement

that your
inner creator
could never
be colonized

—pleasure is liberation too

I want the
river of love
to baptize
us all
to rinse away
every morsel
of shame
and pain
from the fibers
of our beings

I want us
to be free
I want us all
to be free

we are all just trying
to become more
of what we already are

the truth of our desires
already existing in us
pulsing in our haras

can we shift
the focus from
external to internal

and clear the debris
on the pathway
to our hearts

I stand today
on the love
and the hope
contained in the
breath and the bones
of all those who
came before me

I am a
living prayer
the embodiment
of all they wished
I could be

my presence is
a sacred place
my aura a palace
filled with jewels
adorned with precious
rubies and pearls
that sparkle with
lights that illuminate
the darkest corners
and penetrate through
to the deepest shadows

beckoning them forth
with the assurance
of love and
acceptance
a holy space
where even
the lowest of lows
can be alchemized
to heights unfathomed
a promised land
that can be realized

dive deep
baptize yourself
in the sweetness
of my nectar

I am
        both
wild
        and
                holy
completely
            divine

I am
awakening
remembering

a power
that lives
deep within
the nuclei
of my cells

a power
that lives
beyond
this 3D realm
seeded in the
multidimensionality
of existence

a power
that is
our birthright
a boundless
sovereignty
unrestricted
uncontainable
by anyone
but ourselves

awakening
remembering
we are

the seed of
all possibility
anchored
into my womb
shoots lining
up my spine
flowers blooming
out my mouth
in full glory
hallelujah
she's remembered
her divinity

sacred flower
of my vulva
blooming with
pleasure
juicy nectar
dripping from
my petals
folds flourishing
tender with delight

sacred portal
of my yoni
buzzing with the
infinite knowing
of the goddess
she who goes by
a thousand names
and takes a
thousand forms

sacred essence
of my sacral
chakra rooted
in the expansive
field of creation
where seeds
are desires
and the only
watering needed
is love

om
om
om

my womb holds
the sacred seed
the sacred potential
the sacred power
of all creation

om
om
om

—w(om)b

my womb
is life-giving
like the Sun
rays attuning to
another channel
higher frequency
the veil
thinning
the mirages
clearing
the truth
crystalizing
in the height
of the light

—womb(man)

light cannot
be contained
it will always
reach far beyond
its point of origin
baptizing everything
it touches

heart
to womb
love to
the creation
portal

energies
amplifying
unlocking
another flavor
of expression
savored by
the taste buds
of pleasure

heart
to womb
love to
the creation
portal

all is
possible
all is
perfect
covered in
the gracious love
of the mother

sexual energy
the true source
of creation itself
the life force
powering through
us all
supercharging
our abilities
to manifest
our destinies
into reality
birthing forth
new worlds
from pure desire
an eternal play
of possibility
constantly
in motion

the mother of
all life
stemming from
our sacral
sacred and
sexual

pulsing with
desire
to create itself
into more
expressions
of vitality

evidence
that source
is here
electric and
orgasmic
longing for
divine union
with itself

the seeds
of all your
potentials
of all your
expressions

past
                              future
          present

are here
within you
now

building
          blocks
                  conceptions
                              of life
keys to
your own
existence

we are all
master manifesters
creating this world
directly through
our collective
and individual
choices and
agreements

through our
repeated thoughts
and feelings
that spur us
into action
we believe
this world
into being

worlds built
upon worlds

levels upon
levels

connections
and intersections

the micro and
the macro

every perspective
in between

magnifications of
the same workings

a consciousness
experiencing itself

we are coming out of
a deep coma of sorts

we are helping each other
remember who we are

this is
a spiritual awakening

magical illusion
dreaming
while awake

what will
you create

magical illusion
dreaming
while awake

I take a breath
and I escape
back into
no-thing
back into
everything
from which
I came
from which
I am
from which
I will return
from which
I have always
been

magical illusion
dreaming
while awake

what will
you create

have a great life
this one wild chance

you get to be you
in the way that
only you could be you

even if you come back
in another life
it will never be this one

even if you've lived
a thousand times before
it will never be this one

so

have a great life
this one wild chance

you get to be you
in the way that
only you could be you

the surfer does not know which way the tide
will turn. yet they show up and ride the wave
in its ever-changing form. expecting nothing
but a chance to be one with the flow of life.

—Santa Tere II

free
like a soul
who solely
listens to
the resonance
of its own truth

the greatest
act of resistance
living in your
birthright
despite

your heart
the only authority
intuition and
discernment your
only guideposts

love is
a doorway that
I may choose
to walk through
at any time
with anyone
or anything

a friend
a foe
a lover
an aspect
of myself

love is
the wind
and so
I may choose
to leave
the door open
for eternity

so that
there is no
place to go
just a
place to be
free
while love flows
all around me

merkaba
ancient symbol
ancient wisdom

activator
of the light
protector
of the flesh

guided through
the heart chakra
to higher
dimensions

merkaba
a chariot
of love

breathe in
    breathe out

this moment
is perfection

in stillness
is where miracles
are witnessed

the magnitude
of blessings
that exist
in every moment
just beyond
the chaos
of our minds

—the power of presence

I want to be
rooted in love
with you
feet planted
firmly
on the ground

I want to be
rising in love
with you
heart expanding
consciousness rising
higher
into oneness

—divine connections

allow me
to witness
your soul
bare
with no
mask
and no
act

allow me
to witness
your soul
bare
wholly and
true
with nothing
to prove

as I stared
deep
     long
and hard
into your soul
through the stained
glass windows
of your eyes
the world around
started to blur

fading into
the quicksand
of maya
as you and I
became one

one current
of energy
one source
point
one being
extending
into itself

the divine
in different
masks

     —eye gazing

in this hall of mirrors
I am blessed
with sacred reflections
echoing back to me
constantly
my divinity
my humanity
the wholeness
of my being

kundalini
rising up
the ladder
of the
serpent's tree
apple free
truth full
you and I
intertwined
in every
branch and
every vine
pulsating with
divine life
straight from
the source
an invisible
umbilical cord
stringing us
all along
in this
great dance
rasalila
a soulful
love
a great
awakening
a fulfilled
existence

my entire being
is changing
this momentum
that was gaining
and building
energetically
and spiritually
is finally coming
into form and
I am grateful
filled with tears
that brim my eyes
to the point
that at this moment
I can barely see
but I feel
in my heart
and I know
in the movements
of my hands
pressing from
my soul
to the pen
what is true

the truth is
I am in love
I am falling
deeply
in love
with life
with the pure beauty
with the inevitability
of liberation
of love
of joy
of this warm embrace
from which

Sophia hugs me
my tears fall
and I am baptized
again and again
my tears fall
and my heart
breaks free
my tears fall
and new life
is nourished
into being

—eclipse gateway

an integration
after ceaseless ego deaths
harmony achieved

—haiku II

as Venus emerged
from the mouth
of the oyster
bare and celebrated

I emerge
from the chrysalis
birthed into a
new way
of being

cloaked with the
strength of love
blessed with the
innocence of an
uncharted course

allured by
the freedom of
an expression
unscripted

I am
co-conspiring
with the
Great Goddess
with the
Divine Mother
herself

about the author

Vincetta is a poet, spoken word artist, and author of *Metamorphosis* and *The Boundless Bloom*. Writing has arguably been a part of her being since the womb. She has been consciously penning her thoughts and experiences since she can remember.

Inspired by the phrase "feeling over format," Vincetta allows herself to expand beyond a singular medium in order to be a vessel for whatever is wanting to be expressed through her, experimenting with producing soundscapes and photography in addition to writing. She also serves as a ceremonialist and healing guide for the community at Free True You.

You can find more information about Vincetta at vincetta.co. You can also follow her journey on social media at @byvincetta.